POCKET WISDOM
—|FOR|—
INNOVATORS

HANDS ON INNOVATION

Bob 'Idea Man' Hooey
Author of Why Didn't I THINK of That?

I0053724

Updated 2024 – 3rd edition

"Innovation is taking two things that exist and putting them together in a new way." Tom Freston

CREATIVITY

*" Creativity has been built into everyone of us;
it's part of our design.*

*Each of us lives less of the life God intended
for us when we choose not to live out
the creative powers we possess."*
Ted Engstrom

*"Creativity is especially expressed in the ability to
make connections, to make associations, to turn
things around and express them in a new way."*
Tim Hansen

*"One of the major factors which differentiates creative
people from lesser creative people is that creative
people pay attention to their small ideas."*
Roger von Oech

"We do not yet trust the unknown powers of thought."
Ralph Waldo Emerson

*"Nothing is more dangerous than an idea,
when it's the only idea you have."*
Linus Pauling

*"The 'genius' of innovation lies in capturing ideas,
analyzing them, and then confidently moving ahead
to creatively bring them into reality."*
Bob 'Idea Man' Hooey

Growing to the next level (using innovation)

Thank you for allowing me to be a part of your ongoing career enhancement process. As well, for allowing me to play the role of creative *'nudge'* as you explore ways to tap into your creativity and apply innovation in your day-to-day leadership and business roles.

Is your organization stagnating?

Are you finding it a challenge just to keep up with the regular demands made on your team?

Are you being *stretched* financially?

How do you keep growing?

How do you remain competitive?

Growing your people and enhancing their skills will result in growing your organization. Now there is a novel approach to success in business or any viable operation. Making innovation an integral embedded process may just be the answer. After all, you have a process for almost everything else, don't you?

Prepare Yourself to WIN! by investing your time and resources in equipping your team to harness their creativity, to drive innovation, and to grow.

Hands on Innovation (Pocket Wisdom for Innovators) seeks to challenge you to access your creativity, burst your *'locked in'* business bubble and start applying *'systematic'* innovation in your career and operations.

When faced with a challenge or opportunity to grow ask yourself, "What can I…":

Add?
Shrink?
Expand?
Take away?
Adapt?
Modify?
Substitute?
Reverse?
Put to another use?

Perhaps these types of questions should be asked of every facet of your career path or operation with a focus on continually making improvement.

Then take courage, step out, and make any necessary changes. It is when you see your **Ideas At Work** that you truly begin the innovation process.

Bob 'Idea Man' Hooey

Special thanks to my fellow innovators who continue to challenge me to unleash my personal creativity. Special thanks to my wife Irene, my clients, and my fellow authors and speakers who have encouraged and inspired me over the years.

Table of Contents

"Innovation takes birth in sync with the evolution of customer's expectations and demands or vice versa. Either way, organizations around the world have to continually innovate themselves and keep up with the people's wants. The failure to do so or being indifferent to your customer's need will make your competitors win. And then suddenly, customers become indifferent to you- a high-risk gamble to play at."
Ketan Kapoor, Co-founder of <u>Mercer-Mettl</u>

Ideas At Work! – Priming your personal creativity pump

Ever notice how some people seem to be more creative, innovative, or just plain *'lucky'* at discovering solutions or having ideas strike just when they need them?

Ever wonder how they do it or if they were born that way?

Wish you could be more creative?

You can too! Creativity is an acquired mental skill.

There is a secret, *'actually a process'*, which will allow you to access your *'diminished'* creative spark and start a flow of good ideas from which the great, innovative, breakthrough ones might be found. To put it simply, you need to **prime the pump** and be aware of what is happening.

I went camping late one August. A lovely place in Northern Alberta nestled beside a clear, cool lake with lots of trees and natural surroundings. Very rustic and just what I was looking for in my quest to take a mental break from two book writing projects I was working on at the time.

 When I say rustic, *I mean rustic;* **no** *showers, two well-used out-houses, and a fire pit where all that were provided. Water was available via a pump that was connected to a well dug over 100 feet into the ground. It took a lot of pumping, lots of noise, and sweat until a noise was heard coming deep from the earth. Water would eventually gush out. Once flowing, it was easy to maintain the flow while you filled your water container.*

Our minds are like that, deeper than we would expect and often the best ideas are located way down in our subconscious, waiting to be pumped to the surface.

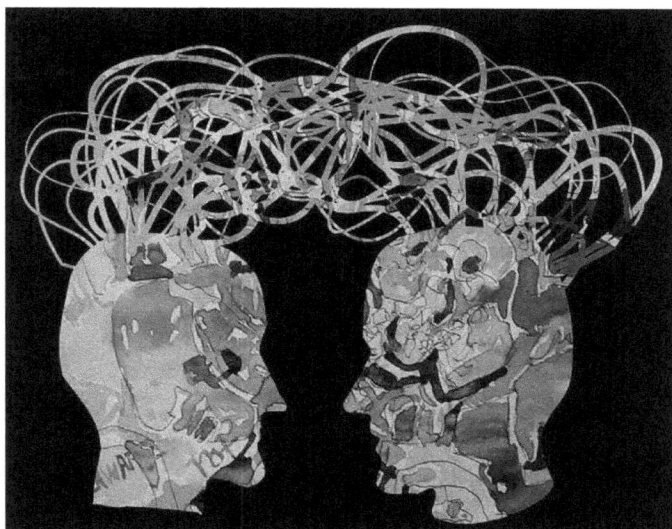

Using your mental muscles is like priming the pump and that is what starts the ideas or water flowing.

Being curious about what is happening around you, reading outside your field, asking questions, *'mining'* or digging into ideas that interest you – all prime the pump and feed the mental reservoir from which the break-through, innovative ideas you seek come from.

Creativity seems easy and it can be if you are systematic at working your brain. Feed your brain the ideas, the challenges, the opportunities, and lots of background, facts and other information and see what bubbles to the surface. **But how do you apply this at work?**

Take a note of some of the other creative people who share in the global market. Perhaps they can teach you something that would be of benefit?

General Electric, under **Jack Welsh**, for example, was famous for *'borrowing'* ideas from other sources. They openly researched ideas that could be transferred to their operations and looked at their suppliers, competitors, their own various divisions, and other companies in the market for inspiration.

If they saw something that was working well, they asked, **"Would this work for us to make us more efficient or more competitive?"** If the answer was 'yes', they would apply it as quickly as it could be put into action.

According to their own history, they learned about productivity from Lighting, quick response asset management from Appliances, and effectiveness from GE Capital.

They learned bullet train cost reduction techniques from Aircraft engines, and global accounting management from Accounting.

Wal-Mart taught them direct customer feedback – quick market intelligence. They learned new product introduction from Toshiba, Chrysler, HP, Toyota, and Yokagaw. Ford and Xerox shared insights on launching quality initiatives.

What have you learned from your competitors, suppliers, or even your own personnel?

Wal-Mart's success is not product specific. Founder, **Sam Walton** looked to others for ideas and was able to apply innovation in his various processes for doing business. Walton applied innovation in supplier relationships, distribution, location, and pricing. This allowed him to maintain a competitive advantage in supplying his customers with what they wanted at a price they could afford.

General Motors was the first automobile manufacturer to introduce color to the product mix, which has had some long-lasting benefit for that industry and for us as consumers.

But did you know they also invented the first form of consumer credit, which allowed people who'd never owned a car to be able to purchase one over time.

3M, famous for inventing the post it notes *(their champion even had to fight to get them introduced as there was no demand at the time, or so the 'experts' said)* has a 30/4 rule in place to encourage its employees to explore new ideas and processes. Simply said, 30% of their sales need to come from products that are less than 4 years old. Keeps them fresh and keeps them priming the creativity pumps.

George **Westinghouse** ran into *'conventional'* wisdom when he suggested to a few railroad executives that a train could be stopped by using wind. His imagination was unstoppable. Westinghouse Air Brakes soon became conventional equipment on North American trains and trucks too.

George de Mestral noticed the burrs he was brushing out of his wool pants and his dog's coat. He became *curious* about the tenacity of the burrs. A little observation under a microscope revealed hundreds of tiny hooks snagged in mats of wool and fur. Years later, he made a brilliant connection and the *profitable* invention of **Velcro™ fasteners** was born.

Albert Einstein would have been proud. Regarding innovation and creativity, he said, ***"To raise new questions, new possibilities, to regard old problems from a new angle, requires creative imagination."***

Three challenges emerge to priming your innovation and creativity pump:

Think things out fresh… be unconventional.

Destroy the old and then create new, where needed.

Tap your imagination. Consider new ideas, ask new questions, and raise new possibilities.

Here is an interesting example.

*Ole Evinrude was in love and engaged to be married. One summer he rowed his fiancée across the lake to a little island for a romantic afternoon picnic. They had forgotten the dessert. Ole rowed back and returned with the dessert. **This was true love!***

About midpoint, tired, beat, and sweating under the sun and humidity, he stopped to catch his breath. Although the ice cream was melting, his creative processes were engaged. He said, **"There must be an easier way to do this!"**

This prompted the invention of the world's first portable outboard motor in 1906, with a commercially successful version in 1909. Ole got his patent in 1910 and went on to dominate the newly developed market for decades.

Creativity can strike when you least expect it. Keep priming the creativity pump and keep your eyes open. You might just surprise yourself and be revealed as a creative thinker and innovator too.

"I believe you have to be willing to be misunderstood if you're going to innovate." **Jeff Bezos, Founder of Amazon**

Food for thought... Feeding your Creativity

Here are a few tips to help you feed your mind and fuel the creative process in your day-to-day role on the job. Use these as mental warm-ups or tune-ups to keep your mind fresh and alive.

Warm up your creativity – take two unrelated objects; imagine comparisons or connections between them. For example, a diamond and an elephant. Both have different facets, and both come from Africa.

Practice mental pinball – take one word or thought; see if you can freely associate 10 - 20 items or thoughts.

Look at other areas, worlds, or industries to spark the solution you need - eg. frequent flyer miles and coffee cards. Hmmm...

Creative environment – create one: for example, casual clothes, a warm room, soft couch, fireplace, soft music, walking outdoors on a lovely day, or working in a dimly lit room can help you.

What would a famous person do? The Pope, Jay Leno, JFK, Mother Theresa, or… *(pick someone you admire for their creative abilities or innovation expertise).*

Think 'POSITIVE' – ie, let's look at the *'workable'* parts. What does work?

Go for quantity if you want quality. Ideas *beget* more ideas! Pick the best ones from the bunch and save the remainder for a reflective look at another time.

Play to keep your creativity alive, *(remember your childhood)*, explore, and have fun with the challenge. Solutions come when you least expect them – **relax and let them come to you!**

Team works – apply the creative power of collective thinking! Create a Success team or un-official team of advisors!

Information, time, and the ability to solve problems creatively are the most **valued currencies** in business.

Learn to use technology, attend a seminar, listen to a tape, read a book, or buy some reactive thinking software.

Innovate or evaporate – The time to act is NOW!
When would be the best time to start some serious work on innovation in your career or organization? **Now!...** is the short answer.

The gap between imagination and creative achievement or actualization has never been shorter. Beginning *'somewhere'* is always preferable to waiting while your team weighs all the options or while the organization goes bust or gets left in the dust by those competitors who are being innovative and creative in this volatile market.

Author of "Leading the Revolution", **Gary Hamel** advocates that ***"radical innovation is the competitive advantage of the new millennium."***

We are facing unprecedented challenges. With the aftermath of 911, the Enron fallout, and more recently Covid-19 global pandemic, and a major shake up in our economy, a wake-up call is in order. That wake-up call creates a serious challenge to productive change with organizations mental constraints and *stuck in the mud* mindsets.

J.K. Galbraith, noted economist once shared, *"Faced with the choice of changing one's mind and proving there is no need to – almost everyone gets busy on the proof."*

12

Everyone needs to be involved. **Partial commitment to innovation is a commitment to failure.** There needs to be a willingness to listen to, and act on, the change plan that comes from this consultative innovation process.

Creative Partners' **Andy Radka** shares the results of a survey of 500 top American CEO's. They were asked what their organization needed to survive in the 21st Century. Their top answer was *"to practice creativity and innovation."*

However, "only 6% of them believed they were tackling this effectively." Quite a large gap between needs and application. Obviously blending in a spirit of innovation takes time vs. a quick fix or special seminar.

If innovation and creativity are so important, even critical in business survival, **why the gap in application and implementation?** While each organization is distinct and different, there needs to be a more holistic, integrated approach to innovation and creativity as a culture. We need to generate *'buy in'* on all levels. Further we need to consider some important points to increase the possibility of idea generation, which in turn drives innovation and creativity in an organization.

What can you do to facilitate this process?

Here are some areas of concern in building a foundation for success under this creative and innovative initiative.

Innovation strategy: Innovation needs to be an *'integral part'* of all strategies and policies in your organization, not just *'tacked'* on as a quick fix up. It needs to permeate every department, every section. Every employee must make it a focus in part as they do their respective roles.

For example, how much time is spent in the boardroom discussing ongoing innovation strategy? This is where the '*rubber hits the road*' and your employees see just how much you are committed to this path of action.

Support from top management: In far too many organizations ideas and innovation steps are already '*at risk*' from their inception. **Leadership** can look the other way or, it can take the courageous step and stretch out a helping hand to buoy them until they can be worked out and tried in the real world.

Ask yourself, "Do my managers see themselves as leaders whose role is to '*clear the way for creativity*' or are they simply status quo oriented?" Your employees and colleagues are watching for your leadership in this arena.

Collective mindsets: Whether we want to acknowledge it or not, we each have mindsets comprised of beliefs, attitudes, and values that drive or motivate our behaviour.

These collective mindsets (*e.g. 'can't teach old dogs' new tricks'* or '*my people aren't creative*') often form barriers to the creative process. They need to be unlocked and unblocked.

Business guru **Peter Drucker** once said, "*defending yesterday – i.e., not innovating – is far riskier than making tomorrow.*"

Ensure sure your organizational mindset is not creating an '*immune system*' or anti-virus system that automatically rejects or attacks new ideas, processes, or challenges to the status quo business model. This thinking is a large obstacle to embedding creative approaches and applied innovation within your organization.

Employees get tools and training: Are your staff given the tools and the on-going training they need to support a creative climate and innovation? People and training are crucial to your success and that training needs to be ongoing and reinforced.

Creativity will not *magically* flourish with the advent of a few courses or the provision of a few creative tools to a few people. Everyone needs to be trained and supported in their evolution of understanding and applied learning.

Knowledge management tools: Does your organization have an intranet that capitalizes on the strides that information technology has brought to the battle for business survival?

IT can act as an enabler, allowing us to break the traditional barriers of function, geography, and even hierarchy. This allows for internet-based sparking of ideas and a chance to engage and bring *'all'* the minds or your various teams into the game.

What gets measured gets done – we need to lay out metrics for innovation: Creativity and innovation can be measured and if so, are done on a more consistent basis. Creativity, when rewarded, even more!

Intellectual assets can impact heavily on your market value. Consider the differential and costs between hardware and software values.

Creation of an idea pipeline:
Is there an effective innovation process, pipeline, or some form of tracking system for converting ideas into innovative services or new products?

Is everyone on your team committed to feeding this process or pipeline?

Only systematic processes, which incorporate a blend of logical and lateral thinking tools can bring creativity and innovation. What are you doing to ensure you *prime the creativity pump* and keep this pipeline full and flowing?

Supplier and customer mindsets: Organizations who create a demand for innovative and supportive suppliers are better able to serve their clients who are, in turn, demanding innovative products and services.

Ask yourself, "Are your current (potential) clients able to support a dialogue about innovating and inventing your shared future?"

How about your suppliers and other allied professionals? They may not even recognize the future *'until they see it'* or are made aware of its possibilities. That, in part, is your job, the connection and education process of business innovation. A few thoughts to consider as you follow your quest to increased creativity and applied innovation in your organization. The time to act is now!

Innovate or evaporate in the dust of those competitors who saw the need, made the   investment, and took the lead. It's your choice!

"Innovation is not a private act – it is seldom the product of a single individual's intellectual brilliance. Innovation is a product of the connections between individuals and their ideas... it is the constant interplay of ideas, perspectives, values and experiences that spawns innovation."
Gary Hamel

Brain Boosters: Give your mind a creative workout! A key to creativity...

Write five unusual fortune cookies

Spend 3 minutes looking around you and noticing everything you see that either has petroleum products in it or was made using petroleum products.

Computer technologists have just launched a new tool. It is called the "birdie". What does it do?

Assume you are blind. Close your eyes, reach into a drawer, and pick up an object that you don't recognize. Describe it using your sound and touch senses.

Write your name upside down — and backwards! This means you have to start with the last letter in your name. Notice how this 'feels'.

On three telephone calls today, guess the age of the person you have talked to, right down to which day and month they were born. (You can even check your accuracy.)

From 'KAI-ZEN' to 'I CAN!' Improvement = Consistent commitment to good change

Kai = *change* Zen = *good*
Used together = *improvement*

Kai-zen came to popularity in North America during the mid-1980's, after becoming an integral part of the Japanese management theory. Western management consultants used it to embrace a wide range of management practices, which were regarded as primarily Japanese. These practices were thought to be the secrets of the strength of Japanese companies in the areas of continual improvement rather than innovation.

According to this theory, the strength of Japanese organizations lay in their attention to process rather than results. They also concentrated the team efforts to continually improve imperfections at each stage of the process. According to them, over the long-term, the result was more reliable, of better quality, more advanced and attractive to clients, and less expensive than Western Management practices.

Its roots however are from an American influence following the 2nd World War. **General Douglas MacArthur** approached several leading US experts to visit Japan to advise them on how to proceed with rebuilding their country and their economy. One such expert was **Dr. Edwards Deming (1900-1993).**

He initially came to Japan to conduct a census but noticed the newly emerging industries were having difficulty. He had been involved in reducing waste in US War manufacturing and drew on that experience to offer his advice. By the 1950's, he was a regular visitor; offering advice to Japanese manufacturers that were having challenges in terms of raw materials, components, and investment; and suffering from low morale in the nation and workforce. By the 1970's, many of Japan's leading organizations had embraced Dr. Deming's key points for management. Most are as valid today as they were a half-century ago.

Key points that relate specifically to the concept called Kai-zen

An improved philosophy to effectively deal with change and client needs.

Constant pursuit of purpose required for improvement of products and services.

Improving every process for planning, production, and service.

Instituting or embedding on-going, on the job training for all staff using a variety of methods and ideas.

Instituting and supporting leadership that is aimed and focused on helping people do a better job. *(Isn't that the true purpose of 21st Century leadership and management?)*

Breaking down the barriers and boundaries that exist within departments and people. *(GE's CEO, Jack Welsh took this one on personally in his style of management.)*

Encouraging education for the self-improvement of every member of the organization.

Top management is committed to improve *'all'* these points, specifically quality and leadership. Adapting the Kai-zen attitude to our western way of doing business requires a 'major change in corporate culture' – **creating a corporate culture that:**

19

Admits openly and honestly there are problems and challenges.

Encourages a positive, collaborative, consultative attitude to solving or overcoming them.

Actively 'devolves' responsibility to the most appropriate or effective level. The person who is in the best position to deal with the challenge or problem needs to have the time, the tools, and the authority to do so.

Promotes continuous skills-based training and development of attitudes.

The Japanese approach has embedded Kai-zen in its hierarchical structural, although it gives substantially more responsibilities within certain fixed boundaries.

Key features of this management approach and focus are:

Attention to process, rather than results: Analyze every part of the process down to the smallest detail, with a view to improving them. Looks at how employee's actions, equipment, and materials can be improved.

Cross-functional management: Management team has an expanded focus to help improve the process and the skills of the people outside the typical western turf wars.

Use of quality circles: and other tools to support their commitment to continuous improvement.

A range of tools have been developed, along the KAI-ZEN concept, to assist companies to make tangible improvements:

Quality Control Circles: groups of people whose primary focus and purpose is to continually improve quality.

Process-oriented management: more attention focused on the 'how' (the process) rather than the 'what' (the task).

Visible management: top executives are being seen, 'walking the job' (management by walking around) and being available to 'see' and consult on each stage of the process.

Cross-functional management: working across functional divides and typical barriers or boundaries to provide more unity, sense of team, and a wider vision that engages and involves everyone.

Just-in-time management: control of stock and other materials and components to avoid unnecessary expenditures.

PDCA: a process of **P**lan, **D**o, **C**heck, **A**ct to assist in solving challenges.

Statistical process control: enable each machine operator or member of a team to control and measure quality at each stage of the process.

In the Japanese approach to Kai-zen, all of these tools are used in a 'holistic' manner. Contrast this to the current western approach where some of these tools are individually introduced as the 'answer' to every problem or challenge; without consideration of the context within which they were designed to work effectively.

Perceived benefits of a Kai-zen type of approach:

Can lead to a reduction of 'wasted' time and resources.

Can increase productivity.

Relatively easy to introduce – requires no major capital investment.

Can lower the break-even point.

Enables organizations to react quickly to market changes.

Appropriate for fast and slow economies as well as growing or mature markets.

However, we face **challenges when introducing Kai-zen** into the western management mind-set.

It can be difficult to achieve Kai-zen in practice, as it requires a complete or major change in attitude and culture. It needs the energy and commitment of all employees. It also requires a substantive investment of time by leaders and their respective teams. Leaders need to 'slow down' and invest their energy to make this mindset work.

It can be difficult to maintain enthusiasm for several reasons. Some see Kai-zen as a threat to their jobs; poor ideas tend to be put forward along with good ideas, which can at times be de-motivating; by implication, there is never complete satisfaction.

Continuous improvement is not sufficient or a stand-alone approach in itself. Major innovation is still needed. There is a danger of becoming 'evolutionary' in focus to the exclusion of being 'revolutionary' or innovation sensitive. Both concepts are important to growth and sustainability.

In this turbulent, global economy, organizations need to look seriously at any and all methods, tools, techniques, and training processes that might help in this quest for growth. Kai-zen's step-by-step approach is in direct contrast to the great leaps forward many organizations experience via the innovation avenue.

It is almost as though we need to develop a 'bi-focal' approach and viewpoint, which is one that encompasses steady, continuous improvement of current processes, products, and services, while looking for and encouraging creativity and innovation in moving the organization to the next level. *I do this in the development of my various training programs and publications.*

Kai-zen should free up time for senior managers to think about the long-term future of the organization, look for new opportunities, and move to a concentration on 'strategic' issues. Kai-zen can support improvement of 'existing' activities; but it will not provide the impetus for the innovation process, which often provides our great leaps forward. Again, a balanced approach is called for here.

It is the role of 'strategic' leadership to take responsibility for the implementation of an effective corporate mission (purpose or soul), reward, and the organizational structure.

It is the responsibility of 'tactical and strategic' managers to model and practice sound leadership, to promote good teamwork, and to work to ensure everyone understands their roles and the process itself.

It is the responsibility of 'everyone' in the organization (from front-line to senior management), to measure themselves and their teams; to identify in quantifiable, measurable terms, areas for improvement; and to generate ideas to change practice and procedures. Then, continue measurement to ensure this improvement has been achieved, recorded, and celebrated.

Each time it is measured, it can be analyzed, and a new standard achieved or set and measured. This is the cycle of continual improvement. (I CAN!)

A typical or **suggested 'cycle' or process**:

Generate ideas
Evaluate ideas
Decide on action
Plan implementation
Design measurement system
Take action (key)
Set new standard
Measure
Analyze
Define problem/desired state
Identify areas for improvement
Generate ideas

Everyone on your team needs to be 'totally' committed to this cycle of continuous improvement.

Each team member must be given the knowledge, skills, and tools to be able to participate fully and enthusiastically. They need to participate, not only within their own respective teams; but also, across the organization as a whole and as a part of a cross-functional team.

For this to become a reality, work must be undertaken to reinforce, encourage, or build the confidence within your staff to take on greater responsibility and make decisions for themselves.

This was the underlying foundation to the work we did in writing and creating **'The Brick Way – It's about ALL of us'** *for a major Canadian Retailer.*

We wanted to send and support the message of each member of their 6000 plus member team taking additional responsibilities and personal leadership over their respective roles. We wanted to instill a new culture and work to create a 'Company of Leaders'. I later wrote **"In the Company of Leaders"**

This reinforcement is crucial to Kai-Zen's success. In addition to specific skills training and use of tools and knowledge, it is important for us to work on the 'climate for change'; to ensure it is embedded in our corporate culture.

The core values within a Kai-zen based approach to which each of us can aspire are:

Trust and respect for every member of the team across the organization, not just his or her own team. (Not just their department, their own specialization, expertise, or level.) Each individual on a team should be able to openly admit any mistakes or failings they've made or exist in their role, and work on doing a better job the next time.

Responsibility is an individual commitment. Progress is impossible without the ability to admit, learn from, and move forward from mistakes.

A few years back, I listened to 'A Power Talk' CD from **Tony Robbins**, *in which he shared his concept of 'CANI' (Constant and Never-Ending Improvement) for use in our day-to-day lives and roles as leaders. He was quite passionate about his commitment to this concept and for its implementation in our daily lives. He advocated a commitment to constant and never-ending improvement.*

I'd like to take a 'robbins-esque' approach and challenge each of you to take a moment to digest what we've discussed about this transplanted US – filtered through Japan approach to management, as a part of your leadership role. I reworded it to a more positive focused **'I CAN'** *acronym.* **Improvement is continual and never ending.**

If you and your team are going to be successful in taking your organization to the next level of growth, each of you will need to get a firm foundation and focus on the process of Kai-zen style continual improvement. This is in addition to your personal leadership in applied innovation or **Ideas At Work!** - as they apply to your changing roles and the teams you seek to lead.

My challenge for each of you: **Develop an 'I CAN!' approach** and attitude to your leadership and team management and to equip and inspire those you would seek to lead. **'Improvement is continual and never ending'** and it starts with me!'

You can use this **'I CAN' Kai-Zen based focus** in your quest to free up time that you choose to reinvest in the lives and skills of those you lead. Enjoy the journey! In the 'Kai-zen' or 'I CAN!' world, the journey is the goal and provides the sense of achievement and satisfaction.
It really works for top performing leaders and their teams as they remain committed to continual improvement in how they leverage their time and enhance their productivity.

Check out https://elevateapp.com/ for some amazing apps you can download. You can learn a language and educational tips in your free time. Creative use of your phone to learn.

"If I had asked the public what they wanted, they would have said a faster horse." **Henry Ford (1863 – 1947), Founder of Ford Motor Company**

Don't let your fears get in the way of accessing your inner creativity and applying innovation...

Fear of being alone

Being abused

Losing the love of the group

Losing the security of habit

Being criticized

Being an individual

Disturbing tradition or going against prevailing thought

Making mistakes

Being seen as a fool

"Software innovation, like almost every other kind of innovation, requires the ability to collaborate and share ideas with other people, and to sit down and talk with customers and get their feedback and understand their needs." Bill Gates

Break Out-of-the-box Thinking

This will *jog* your problem-solving skills. You can often create novel ideas by **NOT** following expectations, rules, regulations, assumptions or long-standing traditions or company history or policy. Go against the grain and the status quo to find the *ultimate* solution you need.

Just for a moment, **remove the speed limits from your mind** and challenge your traditional linear thinking. Ask yourself a few questions to trigger your creative juices. This will allow you to change the way you look at them. A change in perspective can often productively generate a change in your results.

Take a moment and ask yourself:

What if?
If only?
Why not?
Who says?
Does it apply to me?
By whose standards?
Is there another way?

Continue asking yourself:

Let's pretend for a minute we had all the resources, personnel, and time we needed to solve this challenge. What would we be able to accomplish in that case?

Is there a second right answer?
What happens if we do nothing?
What is the best that can happen?
What is the worst that can happen?

How can we benefit or learn from this specific challenge or experience?

Just a few mind joggers to help kick start your thinking.

Take a few minutes and write down some answers that relate to your goal or problem at hand, as they relate to these previous statements and questions.

Using this innovative style of questioning process helps **unlock your creativity**. It is this creativity that holds the seed of your eventual success in reaching your goal or an innovative resolution of your problem.

A final note:

We trust you have found inspiration and gleaned insights from the ideas and words we shared. We trust, too, that you have taken time to reflect on the wisdom contained and how it might apply to your current situation and your commitment to become more productive in your own personal leadership role.

Now it is time to move on to the next idea ... go back to the beginning and work through this **Pocket Wisdom for Innovators** *again or order another in our on-going series.*

Wishing you enhanced success along your path to becoming or remaining a top performing, inspirational leader who creatively touches and changes the lives of others.

As **Jacob Bronowski** wisely wrote, *"The world can only be grasped by action, not by contemplation... The hand is the cutting edge of the mind."* Ideas in your mind need to be put into practice for the innovation to take root – act today to see your **Ideas At Work!**

About Bob 'Idea Man' Hooey

I frequently travel across North America, and more recently around the globe, sharing my **Ideas At Work!**

With the advent of Covid-19, I pivoted to serve my clients online with virtual presentations. Now you can bring me in virtually.

I am fortunate to get feedback and comments from my audiences and colleagues.

These comments come from people who have been touched, challenged, or simply enjoyed themselves in one of my sessions around the globe.

"Thank you, Bob, it is always a pleasure to see a true professional at work. You have made the name 'Speaker' stand out as a truism – someone who encourages people to examine their lives and adjust. The comments indicated you hit people right where it is important – in their hearts. Each of those in your audience took away a new feeling of personal success and encouragement." **Sherry Knight**, Dimension Eleven Human Resources and Communications

"I am pleased to recommend Bob 'Idea Man' Hooey to any organization looking for a charismatic, confident speaker and seminar leader. I have seen Bob in action on several occasions, and he is ALWAYS on! Bob has the ability to grab his audience's attention and keep it. Quite simply, if Bob is involved – your program or seminar is guaranteed to succeed." **Maurice Laving**, Coordinator Training and Development, **London Drugs**

30

"On very short notice Bob cleared his schedule and graciously presented at our meeting when the original Speaker was unable to attend. **Last week Bob set the tone for our two-day BMO leadership meeting and gave us all a motivational lift.** *His compassion and true interest in people was clearly evident, making him very credible. He shared some great stories, has a wealth of experience and knowledge and it was a pleasure listening to him. His down-to-Earth style makes it easier to retain the information presented. He also followed up with additional info and handouts, cementing his message of building bridges, not walls. Fantastic job, Bob, and thanks again!"* **Barbara Afra Beler**, MBA, Senior Specialist Commercial Community, **Bank of Montreal**, Alberta North

"I still get comments from people about your presentation. Only a few speakers have left an impression that lasts that long. You hit a spot with the tourism people." **Janet Bell, Yukon Economic Forums**

"I have been so excited working with Bob Hooey, *as he has given inspiration and motivation to our leadership team members. Both at the Brick Warehouse – Alberta and at Art Van Furniture – Michigan; with his years of experience in working with business executives and his humorous and delightful packaging of his material, he makes* **learning with Bob a real joy.** *But most importantly, anyone who encounters his material is the better for it."*
Kim Yost, CEO Art Van Furniture (retired), former CEO The Brick

"There are different ways to do innovation. You can plant a lot of seeds, not be committed to any particular one of them, but just see what grows. And this really isn't how we've approached this. We go mission-first, then focus on the pieces we need and go deep on them and be committed to them."
Mark Zuckerberg

Bob's Publications

Bob is a prolific author who has been capturing and sharing his wisdom and experience in printed and electronic forms for the past twenty plus years. In addition to the following publications, he has written for consumer, corporate, professional associations, trade, and on-line publications.

He has also been engaged to write and assist on publications by other writers and companies.

Leadership, business, and career development series

Running TOO Fast (8th edition 2022)
Legacy of Leadership (6th edition 2024)
Make ME Feel Special! (6th edition 2023)
Why Didn't I 'THINK' of That? (5th edition 2022)
Speaking for Success! (10th edition 2023)
THINK Beyond the First Sale (3rd edition 2022)
Prepare Yourself to Win! (3rd edition 2017)
The early years… 1998-2009 – A Tip of the Hat collection
The saga continues… 2010-2019 - A Tip of the Hat collection (2020)

Bob's Mini-book success series

The Courage to Lead! (4th edition 2024)
Creative Conflict (3rd edition 2024)
THINK Before You Ink! (3rd edition 2017)
Running to Win! (2nd edition 2017)
Generate More Sales (5th edition 2023)

Unleash your Business Potential (3rd edition 2017)
Maximize Meetings (2024)
Learn to Listen (2nd edition 2017)
Creativity Counts! (2nd edition 2024)
Create Your Future! (3rd edition 2024)
Get to Yes! *Idea-rich introductions to subtle art of creative persuasion in sales and negotiation (2023)*

Bob's Pocket Wisdom series

Pocket Wisdom for Speakers (updated 2024)
Pocket Wisdom for Leaders – Power of One! (2024)
Pocket Wisdom for Innovators (2024)
Pocket Wisdom Business Builders (2020)
Pocket Wisdom for Sales Professionals (2024)

Quick reads (2017-2020) - more to come in 2024

LEAD! *Idea-rich leadership success strategies*
CREATE! *Idea-rich strategies for enhanced innovation*
TIME! *Idea-rich tips for enhanced performance and productivity*
SERVE! *Idea-rich strategies for enhanced customer service*
SPEAK! *Idea-rich tips and techniques for great presentations*
CREATIVE CONFLICT *Idea-rich leadership for team success*
SUCCEED! *Idea-rich strategies to succeed in business, despite global disruptions (2020)*
WRITE ON! *Idea-rich tips and techniques to bring your book into pixels or print (2020)*

Co-authored books created by Bob

Quantum Success – 3 volume series (2006)
In the Company of Leaders (95th anniversary Edition)
Foundational Success (2nd Edition 2013)
PIVOT To Present: *Idea-rich strategies to deliver your virtual message with impact (2020)*

Copyright and License Notes

Pocket Wisdom for Innovators
Hands on Innovation

Bob 'Idea Man' Hooey, Accredited Speaker, Certified Virtual Presenter, 2011 Spirit of CAPS recipient. Prolific author of 30 plus business, leadership, and career success publications. Author, Speaking for Success!

Unattributed quotations or pieces are by Bob 'Idea Man' Hooey

Photos of Bob: Bonnie-Jean McAllister,
www.elantraphotography.com
Dov Friedman, www.photographybyDov.com
Editorial, layout and design: **Irene Gaudet,** Vitrak Creative Services, vitrakcreative.com

Success Publications – *division of Creativity Corner Inc.*
Box 10, Egremont, AB T0A 0Z0
www.successpublications.ca
Creative office: +1-780-736-0009

Each time I sit down to write, or in this case compile, edit, and write, I am challenged to ensure I deliver something that will be of use-it-now value to my reader. I think we did here. I ask myself, **"If I was reading this, what would I be looking for?"** *As well as* **"Why is this relevant to me, today?"**

These two questions help to keep me focused, *help me to remain clear on my objectives; and they help to remind me to dig into my experiences, stories, examples, and research to provide solid information that will be of benefit and help my readers, when they apply it, succeed.*

Pocket Wisdom for Innovators *is my attempt to capture some of the valuable lessons learned over the past 25 plus years, and virtually in the past 6 months, and to share them with you.*

Bob 'Idea Man' Hooey
www.ideaman.net
www.SuccessPublications.ca
www.HaveMouthWillTravel.com

Connect with me on:
Facebook: www.facebook.com/bob.hooey
LinkedIn: www.linkedin.com/in/canadianideamanbobhooey
YouTube: www.youtube.com/ideamanbob
Smashwords: www.smashwords.com/profile/view/Hooey

Acknowledgements and disclaimers

A very special dedication of this piece of myself, to the two people who meant the most to me, my folks Ron and Marge Hooey. Sadly, both my parents left this earthly realm in 1999. I still miss your encouragement and love. I was blessed with the two of you in my life.

*To my amazing wife and professional proof-reader, **Irene,** who loves, encourages, and supports me in my quest to continue sharing my **Ideas At Work!** across the world. Thank you seems so inadequate for your work in helping make my writing better!*

My thanks to the many people who have encouraged me in my growth as a leader, speaker, and engaging trainer in each area of expertise including sales and negotiation. My thanks to a select few friends for your ongoing support and constructive abuse. ☺ You know who you are.

Special thanks to each of my amazing colleagues and friends who have contributed to this little book. Each contributor allowed us to include their piece and retains the appropriate copyright.

We have not attempted to cite in the electronic text all the authorities and sources consulted in the preparation of this manual. To do so would require much more space than is available. The list would include departments of various governments, libraries, industrial institutions, periodicals, and many individuals. Inspiration was drawn from many sources in the creation of this electronic text.

Warning—Disclaimer

This electronic book is written and designed to provide information on more effective sales and negotiation. It is sold with the explicit understanding that the publisher and author are <u>not</u> engaged in rendering legal, accounting, or other professional services. If legal or other expert assistance is required, the services of a competent professional in your geographic area should be sought.

It is not the purpose of this electronic book (manual) to reprint all the information that is otherwise available to sales professionals, negotiators, and sales leaders. Its primary purpose is to complement, amplify, and supplement other texts and reference materials. You are encouraged to search out and study all the available material, learn as much as possible, and tailor the information to your individual needs. This will help to enhance your success in being a more effective communicator online as well as sales leader, or business owner.

Every effort has been made to make this electronic 'primer' as complete and as accurate as possible within the scope of its focus. However, there **may be mistakes**, both typographical and in content. Therefore, this electronic text should be used only as a general guide or primer and not as the ultimate source of information. Furthermore, this electronic manual contains information that is current only up to the date of publication.

The purpose of this 'primer' is to educate and entertain; perhaps to inform and to inspire. The author(s), contributors and/or publisher shall have neither liability nor responsibility to any person or entity with respect to any loss or damage caused, or alleged to have been caused, directly or indirectly, by the information contained in this electronic 'primer' manual or electronic book.

"There is only one thing stronger than all the armies of the world: and that is an idea whose time has come." Victor Hugo

Creative Freedom

Question everything? Does what you're doing...

- ◆ Provide enhanced 'value' to the product or customer?
- ◆ Improve 'quality'?
- ◆ Improve 'productivity' or directly reduce costs?
- ◆ Improve 'two-way communication'?
- ◆ Improve 'service'
- ◆ Add to employee satisfaction, 'motivation' or morale?
- ◆ 'Empower' your employees to act?
- ◆ Encourage 'innovation'?
- ◆ Speed up the 'decision-making' process?
- ◆ Give customers more 'reasons' to deal with you?
- ◆ 'Free up time' to more productively sell or service?

What if it didn't exist?

Is it already being done by someone else?

Is it a 'valid' tradition? Why?

Can another person, department, or company do it better, faster, less expensively, or more easily?

Principles made personal yield powerful results - Ideas At Work!

Excerpt from 'Why Didn't I THINK of That?' by Bob 'Idea Man' Hooey Available from www.SuccessPublications.ca

Visit our website to see other books created by Bob 'Idea Man' Hooey and add them to your success library.

www.ingramcontent.com/pod-product-compliance
Lightning Source LLC
Chambersburg PA
CBHW071530210326
41597CB00018B/2943